The Broomsquire

Adapted for the Stage

THE ORIGINAL AUTHOR

Sabine Baring-Gould (1834–1924) was born in Exeter, the eldest son of Edward Baring-Gould of Lew Trenchard in north Devon.

Educated at Clare College, Cambridge, he inherited his father's estate in 1872, and became rector there in 1881.

He travelled widely, and wrote many novels, theological studies and songs, among them the hymns *Now the Day is Over* and *Onward, Christian Soldiers*.

He also had an interest in folk lore and folk song, and this is reflected in many of his works.

The Broom-Squire is one of his best-known novels, written after a visit he made to the Hindhead and Thursley areas of Surrey, and was originally published in 1896, running to thirteen editions by 1929.

A tale which naturalist David Bellamy has called his 'firm favourite'.

THE ADAPTION

The idea of dramatising *The Broom-Squire* came from a cast member while we were rehearsing for another local community play. She had just read it, and felt it lent itself to our style of drama. Added to which it was set in our local territory on the Hampshire/Surrey border.

Our troupe have performed it several times since then, and in some interesting locations, once in open air on Hindhead Common itself.

It was conceived from the outset as a 'promenade-style' play, to be performed with the audience sharing the space, and in one scene the action, and encourages 'big' performances from the actors.

We have enjoyed performing it immensely, and hope that you do to.

My thanks to Steve White for his help and encouragement in adapting the story, and to members of Headley Theatre Club for their support in premiering the play in 2000, and repeating the experience later.

Cover pictures: Luke Oates as Jonas and Isabelle Glinn as Matabel in a 2013 production by Headley Theatre Club

The Broomsquire

Dramatised from "The Broom-Squire"
by Sabine Baring-Gould
first published as a novel in 1896

John Owen Smith

The Broomsquire
First published 2000
This edition published November 2015

Typeset and published by John Owen Smith
19 Kay Crescent, Headley Down, Hampshire GU35 8AH

Tel: 01428 712892
wordsmith@johnowensmith.co.uk
www.johnowensmith.co.uk

For further plays by the same author see www.johnowensmith.co.uk

ISBN 978-1-873855-34-8

Printed by CreateSpace

Contents

The sailor's grave in Thursley churchyard

Introduction

In September 1786, a lone sailor was murdered on Hindhead Common by three men. This much is common knowledge. But was the sailor alone?

In his book *The Broom-Squire*, the Victorian author Sabine Baring-Gould imagines that the sailor was carrying a baby daughter, and that she had survived the ambush.

From this point, he develops a story of the orphan girl found in the Devil's Punch Bowl by one of the broomsquires who lived there at the time.

Eighteen years later, the finder and the foundling marry. But the circumstances and results of this union lead to a clash of wills — and more.

John Owen Smith
Headley Down
November 2015

This play was first performed in September 2000

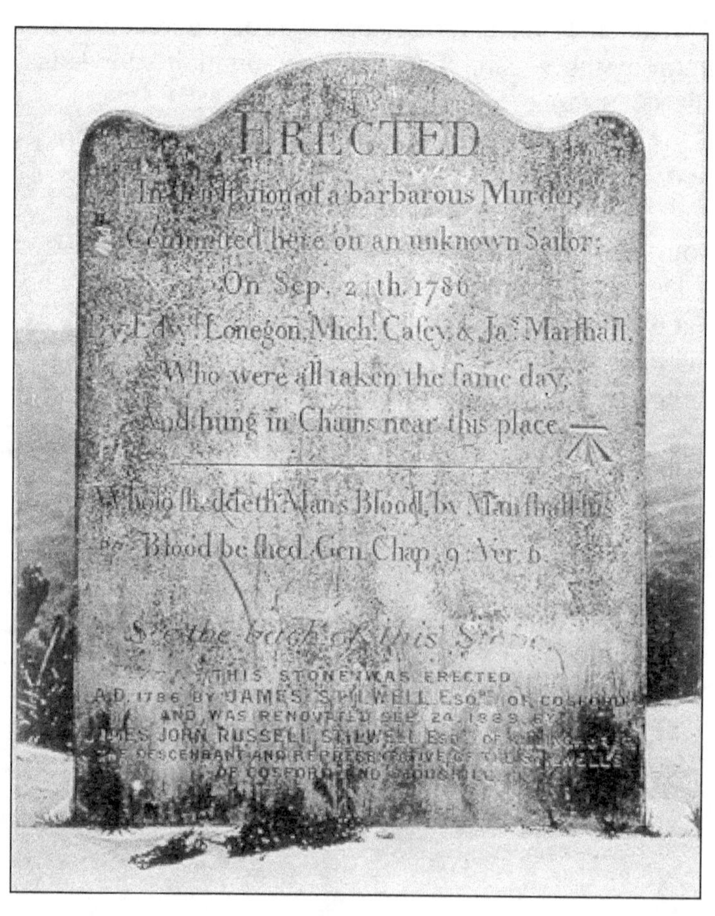

*The Sailor's Stone erected on Hindhead
near the site of the murder*

The Broomsquire

The Broomsquire

Cast List

Matabel .... a foundling
Jonas Kink .... The Broomsquire
Simon Verstage .... Landlord of The Ship Inn at Thursley
Susanna Verstage (Mrs V) .... Wife of Simon
Iver Verstage .... son of Simon and Susanna
Sarah Rocliffe .... sister of Jonas, wife of Thomas Rocliffe
Giles Cheel .... a broomsquire in the Devil's Punch Bowl
Betsy Cheel .... wife of Giles
Markham .... a solicitor
Barelegs .... an attorney
Judge .... at Kingston Crown Court
Defence Counsel .... for Matabel
Puttenham .... Guardian of the Poor in Thursley
Doctor .... staying at *The Ship*
Vicar .... of Thursley
The Sailor .... murdered at Hindhead
Casey .... |
Marshall .... | the sailor's murderers
Lonigon .... |

Labourers, Jurymen, etc

The play takes place 'in promenade' — the space is shared by actors
and audience and represents locations in and around the Devil's Punch
Bowl at Hindhead and Thursley at the end of the 18th century.
    The action is continuous throughout.

List of Scenes

***** Interval *****

Mel White and Tony Grant
play Matabel and Jonas, September 2000

The Broomsquire

<u>Scene 1</u> Introduction

We hear a school bell ringing offstage – Matabel enters still ringing it

Mrs V That's Mrs Kink, the schoolma'am of Thursley …

Simon … Matabel Kink, the old Broomsquire's widow …

Mrs V … who once was Mehetabel, found in the Punch Bowl …

Iver … marked with the gallows …

Jonas … saved from a hanging.

Sarah Some say he tripped …

Jonas …and some say she pushed him …

Simon & Iver … who knows …

Mrs V, Jonas & Sarah … who can tell?

All Only she!

Enter the Vicar of Thursley

Vicar I have been thinking, Mrs Kink, that I should much like to know your system of education. I hear from all quarters such good accounts of your children.

Matabel System sir? I have none.

Vicar None, Mrs Kink?

Matabel None vicar. I just teach what should be taught as a matter of course.

Vicar And that is?

Matabel To love and fear God.

Vicar And?

Matabel That C A T spells cat and D O G spells dog …

Vicar And next?

Matabel That two and two makes four, and three times four makes twelve.

Vicar And next?

Matabel Mine is only a school for beginners, vicar.

Vicar You teach no more than that?

Matabel I lay the foundations on which all the rest can be raised …
by others.

Vicar And you are happy?

Matabel Happy? Oh yes, I couldn't be happier. Except …

Vicar Yes?

Matabel 'Tis no matter.

> *Matabel moves from the vicar towards some children*
>
> *In another place we see a sailor and three other men
> walking up to Hindhead*

Sailor So, Michael Casey, you claim to be one of my shipmates of
old. I can't say I remember you.

Casey It was some time ago. I remember your face well, but not your
name.

Sailor And your friends here, you're all bound for Portsmouth?

Casey Aye, back to sign on again — but we've not been as fortunate
with our money as you have. Ours is all spent.

Sailor Fortunate? With this babby in my arms and her mother dead in
London – that's fortune?

Marshall 'Tis more than we have.

Sailor 'Tis more than I want. As soon as I get her to my wife's sister,
it'll be the freedom of the open sea for me.

Marshall You've enough there to buy us drinks at all the taverns from
here to Portsmouth.

Lonigon And have sovereigns to spare.

Casey So you won't mind sharing it with your old shipmates, will
you?

Sailor There's only one of you reckons to be my old shipmate.

Casey But we're all in this together *(significantly, to Marshall and
Lonigon)* aren't we my brave boys?

Marshall We're with you Michael.

Lonigon Just say the word.

Sailor *(Uneasily)* We agreed to keep each other company on the road, did we not?

Casey So we did. But we'll keep the company, and you can keep the road. *(He draws a knife, and the other two follow suite)*

Sailor Villains!

The sailor is dragged off the road and stabbed – the men take his possessions and run away

Sarah Murderers three, they were caught and convicted …

Simon … hung from the gibbet on top of the hill …

Sarah … and as for the baby girl …

Simon … orphaned on Hindhead …

Sarah … the schoolma'am of Thursley has thoughts of her still.

Matabel I couldn't be happier. Except …

Scene 2 At the Ship Inn

Mrs V He baptised her. That's Iver, my son, he baptised her.
Thought she might die, so he soused her in rainwater.
Gave her a name that he'd heard in the Bible –
Mehetabel – how d'you like that for a mouthful?

Jonas Matabel.

Mrs V Matabel, that's what they called her.
And why couldn't folks in the Punch Bowl look after her?

Jonas Too busy squabbling to take in a babby.

Mrs V T'were you that found her.

Jonas Me? I'm a hudger – you can't 'spect a bach'lor ter take in a babby.

Mrs V So she came to the *Ship*, and we raised her like a daughter.

Jonas Made sure the parish paid her keep though, didn't you? A Charity Girl she were – no daughter of yourn.

Mrs V We raised her like a daughter.

Jonas Aye, and saved on taking a servant too, I'll be bound.

Mrs V Like a daughter.

Jonas And when that son of yours left home …

Simon What d'you mean 'perspective'?

Iver You can't see the side of a ship and the stern of a ship all at the same time – that's what I mean.

Simon She's got a stern, ain't she? So what's we to deny it her?

Iver It's not right. I can paint you a better one.

Simon Listen son, when I want my inn-sign painted, I'll call in a painter to do it.

Iver A painter!

Simon Aye. Now, you stop fiddling with them brushes and start helping me a mite more.

Iver Call in a painter? Like the one that painted it wrong in the first place.

Simon Iver, I warn ye – there's a business and a farm to be run here, and I'll have no lah-de-dah son of mine playing around with a paintbrush when he should be mucking over the fields.

Iver You can muck over your own fields!

Simon What was that?

Iver You heard me.

Mrs V Iver, that's no way to speak to your father.

Iver He's ignorant.

Simon What's that?

Iver He can't understand what's in front of his face.

Simon You'll take that back!

Iver He's dull, stupid and ignorant …

Mrs V Iver, no. Show some respect — please.

Iver … dull, stupid, obstinate and ignorant. *(Exits)*

Simon *(Going after him)* Come here, you …

Mrs V *(Trying to stop him)* Simon, leave him be – he'll get over …

But Simon has gone

Jonas And when that son of yours left home …

Mrs V She's been a great comfort to me, has Matabel.

Matabel Mother, I had a letter from Iver today.

Mrs V To you? Can't he write to his own mother?

Matabel He doesn't want to get you into trouble with father. You
know how he'd be if he saw Iver's handwriting on a letter to you.

Mrs V So, after all this time he writes to you — after how many
months? And is he well, my son?

Matabel He's well … and he's secured himself a position.

Mrs V A position.

Matabel He says he didn't want to write until he'd proved he could
maintain himself.

Mrs V What kind of a position?

Matabel As a drawing master.

Mrs V So, he's not coming home.

Matabel He's doing well, he says. Will you write back to him?

Mrs V I don't have the scholarship to do it easy, Matabel, and that's
the truth.

Matabel Then, shall I?

Mrs V Yes, you write to him, as Mrs Chivers taught you to in the
school. Father won't hear his name mentioned, and you don't know
how it hurts me — all this time without word of my own flesh and
blood. My heart aches for him, Matabel, I can tell you — and
you're the only one I can tell.

Matabel And I'll always be here with you, mother.

<u>Scene 3</u> In the Punch Bowl

Sarah You back from the *Ship* then.

Jonas What's it to you? Keep yer nose to yerself.

Sarah Must be their best customer, the time you spend down there.

Jonas You got your own house to go to, ain't you?

Sarah Sniffing round that girl all the time.

Jonas What girl?

Sarah You know what girl — that Matabel …

Jonas I said, you got your own house to go to!

Sarah … what was found by you abandoned, all them years ago …

Jonas You're only my sister — you got no rights to criticise …

Sarah … an outsider, marked by the gallows she is …

Jonas … what I do, or where I go, or who I see …

Sarah … and grown up into a proper little hussy …

Jonas … it's me own business, see?

Sarah … out to get her hands on your money.

Jonas I says, you're only my sister — what's it to you?

Sarah Cast yer net outside the Punch Bowl and you'll regret it, Jonas Kink.

Jonas I knows your mind, Sarah Rocliffe — you thinks you'll inherit all my wealth if I die single, isn't that the fact?

Sarah You'd never have looked after yourself, not after our mother passed away — not without me round to help you every day. Like a wife I was to you.

Jonas Help — that's what you call it! Sticking yer nose into every corner of my affairs.

Sarah That house of yours'd be unfit to live in now if it weren't for me.

Jonas You want me a bachelor, want me a hudger,
just so's you'll inherit — you and your husband …

Sarah Least he's from the Bowl — he's not an outsider …

Jonas … and here you are snooping and prying around again.

Sarah … not like that Matabel down at the inn.

Jonas So now, I've got news for you — let's see your face —
you see, I'm a-minded to get myself married …

Sarah Not to her? Don't tell me you've already asked.

Jonas Maybe yes, maybe no — you'll have to discover.

Sarah I'll see you in hell first!

Jonas Who knows, sister dear?

Scene 4 At the Ship Inn

Simon Fine haymaking weather. Fancy I'll carry it all in tomorrow.

Mrs V Simon, will you answer that letter now?

Simon What letter?

Mrs V You know very well what letter – Iver's letter.

Simon Pah!

Mrs V Now he's written to you himself – he wants to square it with
you.

Simon A drawing master! My son a drawing master.

Mrs V He's got into a good business. He sells his pictures at
Guildford. It's but a matter of time and he'll be famous.

Simon I'd as soon he played the fiddle and taught dancing.

Mrs V How can you say that?

Simon Because it's how I feels. Here he had a good farm and a good
inn – good businesses that don't dwindle. And yet off he went,
chucked aside the blessings of Providence, to take up with
scribbling and scrawling on paper.

Mrs V Simon …

Simon I don't see why I should werrit about him or any other thing. I'll just put my feet up and enjoy myself.

Mrs V I pray you, answer his letter.

Simon I shall not.

Matabel is about to enter, but stops

Mrs V Iver's your son, your only child. He hadn't the gift to be a farmer, but he had to painting. It can't be other – Providence orders all.

Simon That's all gammon.

Mrs V We're getting old. In the end you'll have to give up work, and who but Iver comes after you here?

Simon You says yourself he's not fit to be a farmer.

Mrs V Then he may let the farm and stick to the inn.

Simon He's just about fit for nothing at all.

Mrs V Indeed but he is, only not in the way you fancies.

Simon All the money you and I've scraped together, he'll chuck it away with both hands.

Mrs V He may marry a thrifty wife – as you have done.

Simon And live by her labour? That a child of mine should come to that!

Mrs V Iver's your own flesh and blood – how can you be so hard on him? You can't leave everything to a stranger.

Simon I can do what I will with my own. What hinders me leaving the whole lot to Matabel?

Mrs V You ain't speaking serious, Simon.

Simon You've had that girl with you in place of a child all these years. Don't she thoroughly understand the business? Has she ever left the hogs unmeated or the cow unmilked?

Mrs V I don't deny Matabel's a good girl, but …

Simon I might do worse. She'll marry a good man as'll look after the farm, and she'll mind the public house. Better than leave it to that wastrel son of ours.

Mrs V He was a boy then. He's a man now.

Simon He's still a dauber of paints. *(Rising)* I'll go and cast an eye over the hay field – it makes me all of a rage to think of him.

Simon exits, and Matabel enters

Matabel It's so hot in the kitchen, mother. I thought I'd come out to cool myself. *(Pause)* Where's father? I thought I heard him talking to you?

Mrs V He's gone out – and he won't answer Iver's letter. He's as hard as Thor's Stone.

Matabel No, mother, he's not hard. But he won't like to give way all at once. You write to Iver and tell him to come home. Father won't hold out when he has his own son here in front of him.

Mrs V Did you hear all that father and I were saying?

Matabel I heard him call out against Iver.

Mrs V Nothing else?

Matabel Saying he'd never make a farmer.

Mrs V It's a dratted nuisance in this porch – acts like an ear to the house. You sure you heard no more?

Matabel I was busy mother – I didn't pay attention to what didn't concern me.

Mrs V Oh, only listened to what did concern you, did you?

Matabel Mother, write to Iver – it needn't be many words.

Mrs V Won't make no difference – his father's resolute.

Matabel But he's tender-hearted under it all.

Mrs V Oh yes, so long as he ain't crossed he's right enough. *(Pause)* Matabel, whatever father may have said about making a Will, it's all gammon and nonsense. He has only Iver. The law will see that everything goes to Iver, just as it ought.

Matabel You will write to Iver to come?

Mrs V Aye, I will. Matters can't get worse by it. How I've suffered all these years, parted from my only child!

Matabel I have tried to do what I could for you, dear mother.

Mrs V Oh yes, that I know well enough. But you ain't my flesh and blood. You may call me mother, and Simon father, but that doesn't alter matters. You can call cabbage plants cauliflowers, but it don't make them grow flower heads. Iver is my own son, my very own child. You, Matabel, are only …

Matabel Only what, mother?

Mrs V … only a charity girl. *(Exits)*

<u>Scene 5</u> Jonas proposes

Matabel Only a charity girl? But I thought … you loved me. So after all these years, I still have no father and no mother — no name to call my own except the one given to me in charity — I owe my clothes to charity, my food to charity, *(she wipes away a tear)* even this handkerchief to charity.

Jonas is moving towards the Ship

Jonas A-minded to get myself married … and who better than a girl with no other prospects …

Matabel I've heard the words often enough at school — but never from mother before.

Jonas … a girl in need of a home and a man to look after …

Matabel rises and prepares to go out

Matabel I'll go to meet father coming back from the fields — perhaps he'll have a kinder word for me.

Jonas … a girl fit to bear children — and serve my sour-faced sister aright …

He sees Matabel emerge from the Ship

… and a handsome girl too.

(To Matabel) I'm glad to have caught you — and caught you alone.

Matabel What do you want, Jonas?

Jonas I want you, Matabel.

Matabel Want what with me?

Jonas Want what? I care more for you than for anyone else.

Matabel That's not saying much.

Jonas I care for you alone in the world.

Matabel Except for yourself!

Jonas Of course. *(aside)* I've not been a marrying man – a wife and
family cost too much.
Been saving, not spending, but it can't go on for ever – All good
things must come to an end.

Sarah Marrying outside the Bowl. Who's she? A charity girl from
the village – a brazen hussy.

	You can't break the rule, Jonas –
	You can't break *(overlap with Jonas)* the rule.
Jonas	*(overlap with Sarah)* My sister, the bane of my life – she thinks she'll inherit if I stay a hudger, but beggar her luck – I'll marry to spite her.
Sarah	You can't break the rule.
Matabel	You want me for housekeeper.
Jonas	Housekeeper? No. I want you to marry me – fair and respectable. Didn't say 'housekeeper'.
Matabel	So you can make a long nose at your sister and keep her away from you – keep her away from
M&S *(together)* you –	
Sarah	can't break the rule.
Jonas	*(Aside)* So I'll spread out my net – and just like the rabbits, there you'll be, pretty and plump for the taking.
Mrs V	He asked you to marry him.
Matabel	Can you believe it? Snared in his trap, and he thinks I'll be grateful. Be grateful!

Mrs V	To marry him.
	Well, there are worse.
	Though I'll grant you he's too good a customer here
	at the inn. But a good wife will cure him of that.
	A hudger does things as a married man doesn't.
Matabel	A wedding won't bring out good stuff from a toad.
Mrs V	Who says there ain't maybe some good stuff in Jonas?
Matabel	I've not seen a glint of it.
Mrs V	Nor you don't see gold lies under the sand.
	But there it is waiting for someone to find it,
	and claim it ... and work on it.
Matabel	He can find someone else, for I don't want him.
Mrs V	There's many men's character just like their waistcoats,
	all satin in front, but the back's patched with calico –
	That's not your Jonas …
Matabel	<u>My</u> Jonas?
Mrs V	Aye, Mattee,
	your Jonas. For you'd be a fool not to take him.
	His worst side is foremost, I like that in men.
Matabel	I'd as soon take the Devil!
Jonas	She'll take me, and grateful –
	you'll see if she doesn't.
Sarah	The rule of the Punch Bowl –
	you marry your own folk –
	no place for outsiders,
	they only bring hardship,
	they only bring trouble –
	you marry your own folk,
	be warned Jonas Kink.
Jonas	I'll marry my choosing, you sour-minded cow.
Mrs V	What good's there in waiting when all's in agreement?
	You marry for money, not love, in this world.

Matabel	But mother …
Mrs V	For money.
	You know that we love you,
	but …
Matabel	Yes?
Mrs V	… for all that, you're

Mrs V & M (*together*) a Charity Girl.

Matabel	So I'm to be thrown to the first man who'll have me.
Mrs V	Now Mattee …
Matabel	The first man to show any interest.
	I wasn't aware I was quite such a burden.
Mrs V	We love you …
Matabel	… but not as your own flesh and blood.
	I understand – <u>mother</u> –
	I understand now.

Jonas	They're reading the banns, and it's three weeks on Sunday.
Sarah	The folk from the Bowl won't be there if they're asked.
Mrs V	We'll have food and drink at the inn for all comers.
Matabel	And Matabel Kink gets a surname at last.

Together:—

Sarah	A charity girl –
	she'll only bring hardship,
	she'll only bring trouble –
Jonas	A charity girl –
	she'll bring me no hardship,
	she'll bring me no trouble –
Mrs V	A charity girl –
	she'll bring you no hardship,
	she'll bring you no trouble –

Matabel	A charity girl – I'll know about hardship, I'll know about trouble –

Sarah	You'll make her your mistress,
Jonas	I'll take her for mistress,
Mrs V	You'll soon be the mistress,
All	*(Loud)* **Of sly Jonas Kink!**

Sarah	A hornet lived in a hollow tree, A proper spiteful twoad were he, And he said as married he'd happy be, But all the folks jeered and laughed at he!
Jonas	*(To audience)* All good things must come to an end.

Jonas guides Matabel from the stage, none too gently.
Lights fade on the scene.

<u>Scene 6</u> The Wedding party at the Ship Inn

Labourer 1 Jim, the old hornet out of the hollow tree be in luck today! What'll he do with her, now he's catched a butterfly?

Labourer 2 What'll he be like to do with her?

Labourer 1 A proper spiteful twoad such as he — why he'll rumple all the colour and beauty out of her wings, and sting her till her blood runs poison.

There is general merrymaking, during which Jonas & Matabel arrive from the wedding. At some point we see Simon giving Matabel a small bag of money, without Jonas noticing.

Simon Best go easy on that drink, Jonas, or you'll never get your new wife home tonight.

Jonas S'my wedding, landlord — and I've a mind to sing you all a song. "Oh a cobbler there was, and he lived in a stall …"‡

Simon Now, look here, we all of us know that there ballet pretty well. It's vastly long if I remembers aright, and I think we can do very well without it today.

Mrs V There's more roast duck and green peas for all.

Jonas For all? Don't see too many of my own folk here.

Mrs V They were asked, Jonas. 'Taint my fault if they choose not to turn up.

Jonas 'Tis one thing if they're not at the church, but surprising they don't come for the feast. Roast duck and green peas! *(To Matabel)* But it don't matter a rush — we can get along without them. Come, say a word of thanks. Better late than never. At last, through me, you've got yourself a surname.

Labourer 1 Taking his butterfly back home.

Labourer 2 To rumple her wings.

Jonas What d'you mean by that?

Matabel *(Trying to avoid a fight starting)* Jonas, no!

Labourer 1 Marrying outside the Bowl.

Labourer 2 It's an ill bird befouls its own nest.

Jonas Was that aimed at me?

Simon We'll have no brawling here today. Stand back!

A brawl is about to start when Iver enters

Mrs V Iver? It's Iver — my son Iver, he's back! *(They embrace)*

Simon Who?

Matabel *(To Simon)* Dear father, this is my wedding day. I am about to leave you for good. Don't deny me my only request. Forgive Iver.

---

‡ The actor playing Jonas may sing whatever ribald song he knows, maybe standing on the table

Iver *(To Simon)* See, I am free to admit, and do it heartily, that I was wrong in painting over the stern of the ship. But I can put things to right for you. For you, I'll violate all the laws of perspective in heaven and earth and make that precious vessel look like a dog curling itself up for a nap. Will that satisfy you?

Mrs V Simon, he's your own flesh and blood.

Matabel Father, for my sake.

Simon *(To Iver)* There is my hand.

Iver And you shall have the sign again just as it suits you.

Simon It'll be easier to get the old ship to look what she ought, than to get you to look like a publican's son again.

Iver *(Looking at Matabel)* Heaven bless me, and what is the meaning of all this?

Mrs V That is young Matabel, as you baptised, them eighteen years ago — and this is her wedding day.

Iver My little pen pal. You, married? And today, the day of my return! Where is the happy man? — show him to me!
(It becomes apparent to him it is Jonas) What! Bideabout the broomsquire? Never, surely! So you have won the prize — you!
(He does not extend his hand to Jonas, but going to Matabel, holding her hands) And little Matabel — I have returned too late — to lose you. I wish you joy. I wish you everything — everything that your heart can desire. My little Matabel, grown so handsome — and, hang me, leaving the *Ship*.
Bideabout, I should have been consulted. I baptised her — I have certain rights over her, and I won't surrender them in a hurry!
Here, mother, give me a glass — 'tis a strange day on which I come home.
(Raising his glass) Here's to you, Matabel — may you be very happy — with the man of your choice.

Jonas And have you no good wish for me?

Iver For you, Bideabout, I do not express a wish. I know for a certainty that you — that any man — must be happy with such a girl — unless he is a cur!

<u>Scene 7</u> At Jonas's house

Jonas and Matabel arrive from the wedding feast

Sarah I thought you were never coming. Goodness knows, I have enough to do in my own house without being kept waiting because others find time for making fools of themselves.

Jonas I'm going to stable the horse. You women can sort out your own domestics.

Sarah *(After him)* And I hope I shall not be wanted longer. My man needs his meals as much as others, and if he don't get them regular, who suffers but I? Duty begins at home. You might have had more consideration and been home earlier, Jonas.

Jonas *(Away)* Could have come yourself if you'd wanted.

Sarah *(To Matabel)* I didn't light a fire. It wouldn't do, not now you're here as mistress. I've heard tell it's unlucky for any other body to do it. Not as I knows, mind.
I didn't lay out nothing either. I supposed you'd had as much as is good for you where you've come from. Roast duck and green peas, so I heard tell. But if you're hungry there's cold rabbit pie in the larder, if it ain't gone off — bad weather for keeping meat. And the rats got the bread because Jonas wouldn't cover it up after his breakfast. There's ale in the barrel, I know, but Jonas keeps the key to that. And he expects me to work for him like a galley-slave.

Matabel What's that noise?

Sarah The sow in her pen, wanting her meat. She ain't been gallivanting around like some today, and she'll be going back in her flesh unless she's fed pretty smart. You'd best get acquainted, and the sooner the better. She's regular rampageous with hunger.

Matabel Would you help me with my box, Mrs Rocliffe? If I can get it indoors I'll change and get on with things.

Sarah I've such a terrible crick in my back, I dussn't do it. How much does it weigh? I wonder Jonas had the face to put it on the cart and expect Old Clutch to draw it.
Ducks and green peas! Don't you reckon on eating that every day here, nor on Sundays, nor even at Christmas. 'Tain't such as we in the Punch Bowl as can stuff ourselves on ducks and green peas.

Green peas and ducks we may grow — but we sells 'em to the quality.
I'll go and get my son Samuel to help you with the box — he's probably idling, he mostly is.

Sarah goes, and Matabel starts to inspect the premises
— Sarah suddenly returns

And you'd best set to work making some gruel for Old Clutch — he'll be off his meat what with drawing such a weight — and Jonas can't afford to lose him just because he's got a wife now. *(Exits)*

Matabel continues to inspect the room — then she looks for her bag of money and finds it gone

Matabel Jonas! Jonas, I've been robbed!

Jonas *(Entering)* Robbed? What's up?

Matabel The money which father gave me — it's gone.

Jonas That fifteen pounds in the little bag?

Matabel I'm not accustomed to pockets, so I tucked it away — it must have fallen out on the way here.

Jonas I told you to give it to me.

Matabel Father said not to let it out of my hands.

Jonas Didn't you swear in church to endow me with all your worldly goods?

Matabel No, it was you who did that. I had nothing then.

Jonas Oh, was it so? I don't remember that.

Matabel Jonas! You took it! You robbed me on the road there, at the same spot those men robbed my father.

Jonas See here, Matabel, and mind what I say. In matrimony it's all give and take, and it'll be a bostal road with you and me unless there's give on one side and take on the other.

Matabel Is all the give to be on my side and the take on yours?

Jonas Of course — what else is matrimony? And the sooner you learn that, the better for peace. I ain't going to have this other than Paradise if I can help it.

<u>Scene 8</u> Mrs V and Iver visit Matabel & Jonas in the Punch Bowl

Mrs V and Iver approach Jonas's house

Mrs V I miss her at the *Ship*, that much I'll own to.

Iver She'll be happy to see you, and show you round her new home.

Mrs V And the dull-head of a maid that's replaced her — broken three pots already.

Iver And now Jonas the broomsquire has what you let go.

Matabel Mother, you've come. *(She and Mrs V embrace)*

Jonas Ah, Mr Iver — over here. I've been wanting a word with you. *(Jonas and Iver move away)*

Mrs V *(To Matabel)* It's a fair decent house you've got. All yours, not rented. And how are you coping?

Matabel Not bad. Do you miss me?

Mrs V I did you a favour to push this one on, eh? And he'll have a nest-egg stuck away somewhere, up in the chimney or under the hearth — that's the way in the Punch Bowl.

Matabel He keeps all his in the Wealden Bank — he's that much of a skinflint. I said, do you miss me?

Mrs V I remember old Boxall tried taking his with him — stuffed in his mouth it was, and him a corpse.

Matabel Yes, mother, I'd heard that. I asked, are you missing me?

Mrs V Missing you? No, dear, for that would be selfish — it's all for your good — this is just how it ought to be. *(She moves away)*

Jonas So, you're a painter. Is that a profession?

Iver What do you mean?

Jonas I mean, does it pay?

Iver That depends how you judge it. How much are your brooms?

Jonas Three shillings a dozen — the best that you'll find.

Iver Well then, let me think. The last painting I sold fetched me –
two hundred brooms.

Jonas How much?

Iver Two hundred brooms, thereabouts.

Jonas I've been thinking — you say you've a mind to do sketches
down here in the Punch Bowl?

Iver That's right.

Jonas So it seems only fair that I takes a percentage if they shows my
property.

Matabel *(Aside)* Can I believe it? He wants to charge money!

Jonas Matabel here — she can pose really pretty in front of the
spring, holding a pitcher — should make a good picture. I daresay
you'll sell it …

Iver I dare say I will.

Jonas … and give us commission. *(Exits)*

Matabel The mean-minded, grasping … *(to Iver)* I hadn't intended to
speak out so plainly.

Iver I'd rather take you and the pitcher away from him.

Matabel That you must not do! *(Quickly)* "I Mehetabel take thee
Jonas to be my wedded husband to have and to hold from this day
forward for better for worse for richer for poorer in sickness and in
health to love cherish and obey till death do us part amen."

Iver *(cutting in)* I wish you were back in the *Ship*, the old *Ship* — it's
no longer the place of my fond recollections — not now you are
gone.

Matabel You must not speak so, Iver.

Iver Why did you leave? It's strange altogether — my mother not
mentioning …

Matabel Mentioning what?

Iver That you were to wed — no word in her letters. It's almost as if
… it was done precious quickly — she told me to wait before I
came back.

Matabel To wait?

Iver For my father to say he'd accept me. Just half a day earlier —
    that's all it needed to save you from …

Matabel Iver!

Iver To save you from him! *(He goes to kiss her, and she resists)* We
    are brother and sister — where is the harm?

Sarah is watching this — she coughs

Sarah It's early days yet to be starting this kind of thing.

Matabel What do you mean?

Sarah Oh nothing, I'm sure.

Matabel Iver is here.

Sarah Yes — but Jonas, he isn't.

Matabel No, he's gone to Squire Mellers — on business.

Sarah I see.

Matabel Won't you come in? We're just sketching a picture.

Sarah A picture? Two's company, three makes a crowd. Tell Jonas I
    called.

Back at The Ship

Iver It's a puzzle to me which I can't unravel — why Matabel married
    the broomsquire at all.

Mrs V And why should she not? She'd no prospects else. No name,
    no dowry.

Iver No love for the man.

Mrs V Love? That comes second'ry — she'll live to thank me for
    pushing her on to him.

Iver You?

Mrs V And why not? I did my duty — thought of her future. She's
    no child of mine and she's marked with the gallows …

Iver The gallows — because some men murdered her father?

Mrs V It's all one — she's lucky to've picked up the broomsquire.
    Young men, they don't court a girl with her history.

Iver I would have taken her.

Mrs V That's what concerned me!

Simon You're a fool, old woman. We might have been happy if you hadn't meddled about.

Mrs V What d'you mean?

Simon That Matabel, she could have married our Iver, and we'd have had peace in our old age.

Mrs V But Simon …

Simon You can't turn a stream to run up hill — you'll souse your own field and ruin your crops, and there'll be the devil to pay.

Iver I had a dream.

Matabel What did you dream?

Iver Of whom did I dream? I dreamt of you.

Matabel What was your dream?

Iver I dreamt of your marriage.

Matabel Then that means death — but death for who?

Jonas *(entering)* Matabel!

Matabel What do you want with me, Jonas?

Jonas I want you to go to the *Ship*. That Susanna Verstage has fallen out with her new maid, and there are three gentlemen come for the shooting to be attended to. We agreed a shilling a day for you.

Matabel Never!

Jonas I tried to screw more out of her, but …

Matabel Jonas, I do not wish to go.

Jonas But I choose that you shall. With tips you could get half a guinea over the three days …

Matabel I pray you, allow me to stay here …

Jonas And what with that Mr Iver leaving today too, for his shop in Guildford, I reckon she's proper put out.

Matabel Iver, leaving? …

Jonas So you will go, won't you?

Matabel Yes — yes, I will go.

<u>Scene 9</u> At the Ship Inn

Mrs V You packed for Guildford?

Iver Near enough.

Mrs V I daresay Jonas will take you there. He'll be here directly.

Iver Jonas? What's he coming this way for?

Mrs V Never you mind. Get your bags ready.

Iver You seem in some haste to get rid of me again, mother.

Mrs V Haste? No — but it don't go well keeping him waiting.

Iver And here he is. I'll pick up my traps. *(Exits indoors)*
Jonas and Matabel enter from outside

Mrs V You're a good girl, Matabel — I knew you wouldn't say no.

Jonas Shilling a day, we agreed.

Mrs V We did.

Jonas You made the parish pay for her when you took her in, so now
you want her, it's your turn to pay. In advance, is it?

Mrs V And will you take Iver to Guildford with you?

Jonas Thought he'd already gone. There's a pickle. I don't know
that I can.

Matabel He's here still?

Mrs V Not for long, he won't be.

Jonas I've promised to pick up Lintott, and there ain't room in the
trap for more than two.
Iver enters with baggage

Iver Is there a problem?

Mrs V Well I …

Iver Matabel! No-one told me you were coming.

Jonas I must be on my way. Old Clutch is slow enough as it is without wasting time exchanging pleasantries. *(To Mrs V)* Shilling a day then. *(Exits)*

Matabel *(To Iver)* But you are leaving.

Iver True, I was. But Bideabout has gone without me — and now, hang me if I don't delay my departure for a day or two. And you may model for me again.

Mrs V She'll be otherwise employed. I can't spare her for any of that nonsense.

Iver In any event, I shall put my luggage back where it came from. *(Exits indoors)*

Business here, to indicate a lapse of time

Mrs V *(To Matabel)* I dare say you find it lonely at times in the new home — you'll be glad to be back here for a few days where there's plenty going on. How does the broomsquire treat you?

Matabel *(After a pause)* Jonas is not unkind.

Mrs V You can't expect love-making every day. It's the way of men to promise the sun, moon and planets till you're theirs, and after that the poor woman must be content with the spark off a falling star. I acted for the best — I sought your happiness. Don't tell me that you're unhappy.

Matabel Who is happy? I said he is not unkind. I had no expectation of finding Paradise in the Punch Bowl.

Mrs V With the best intentions, things don't always turn out as expected. All my life I've wished to have Iver by me. He went away because he wanted to be a painter; he's come back after many years and I find him not all I desire. Now he's going away again. He's not the same as he was.

Matabel He is no longer a child. He has something else now to fill his heart beside a mother.

Mrs V *(Nervously)* What's that?

Matabel His art.

Mrs V exits — and soon after, Iver enters

Iver Did you see, Matabel, I've redaubed the old sign quite to father's satisfaction.

Matabel You are going to Guildford tomorrow morning, are you not?

Iver I don't know.

Matabel You have your profession to attend to.

Iver How can I go, with you here?

Matabel Iver, I pray you, be more loving to your mother. You have made her heart ache.

Iver I love mother — of course I love her.

Matabel Not as truly as you should, Iver. She's failing in health, you can see that.

Iver She has done me a cruel wrong.

Matabel She has never done anything to you but good, and out of love.

Iver She has stabbed me through you. Why do you plead her cause when she thrust you into this hateful marriage.

Matabel No, Iver — talk of something else I beg you.

Iver Of what?

Matabel Of anything.

Iver Of my dream then. What I dreamt was, that you and I had married, not you and Jonas — but as I looked at you, your face was deadly pale, and the hand I held was cold as clay.

Matabel There's some truth in it, Iver. You hold a dead girl by the hand. To you, I am, I must be, for ever — dead.

Iver Nonsense. All will come right somehow.

Matabel Yes, for you it will. You are free to love and marry a girl worthy of you in every way. As for me, my lot is cast in the Punch Bowl.

Iver Matabel!

Matabel I am speaking plainly because there is no good in not doing so. Do not make my part more difficult. There is but one thing for us both — we must part and meet no more.

Iver No!

Matabel Be a man — go.

Iver Matabel! It shall not be, it cannot be! My love! My only love!

He tries to grasp her — they struggle

Matabel Let me go! Let me go!

Matabel flees the house

Mrs V What was all that? Where is Matabel? — Where is Matabel?

Iver Gone, mother — gone!

<u>Scene 10</u> To Thor's Stone

Jonas is leaving his house when he meets Sarah

Sarah Where are you going off to? And with a gun too.

Jonas Catch a stag. I hear there's one escaped from the park at Peper Harrow.

Sarah Should have thought you'd best have gone after your own wife, and brought her home.

Jonas She's all right — she's at the *Ship*.

Sarah I know she's at the *Ship*, just where she ought not to be.

Jonas Why not? She'll earn a little money.

Sarah Oh, money! What fools men be!

Jonas What's you on about now?

Sarah You've had Iver Verstage here — you invited him over to paint your Matabel — and he's been admiring her, and saying soft things to her — I've seen it with my own eyes. And now you've sent her to the *Ship*!

She makes a sign to him indicating infidelity

Jonas If you think to mock me, you're all wrong. I know well enough what I'm about. He's gone off to Guildford.

Sarah How do you know that?

Jonas 'Cause Sanna Verstage said as much.

Sarah *(Laughs cruelly)* Did she indeed! Well I don't believe that he's gone.

Jonas Sanna Verstage don't tell lies.

Sarah If he were gone, Matabel wouldn't be so keen to go there.

Jonas She wasn't keen. I had to force her to go.

Sarah She was keen — she just pretended to you she wasn't.

Jonas Hold your slanderous tongue! I'll not hear another word.

Sarah Then you must shut your ears to what the whole parish is saying.

Jonas *(Going)* … I'll hear no more!

Sarah I tell you, he's still there at the *Ship*.

At the Ship, Iver prepares to give chase to Matabel

Mrs V Gone, you say? Where?

Iver Towards the common.

Mrs V Then you'd best get after her. The day's drawn to a close — she's not dressed proper, and that's no place for her to be wandering after dark.

Iver She could have gone anywhere.

Mrs V No, with her mind in the state it's in, she'd only be going to one place. Thor's Stone, over by Pudmore. She'll be going to talk to the Pucksies there.

Matabel is heading for the Thor's Stone,
holding a fist-sized piece of ironstone

Matabel No! I can stand it no longer. He must go! He must go! …

Jonas, in her path, thinks he hears a deer approaching

Jonas Ah, the stag. *(He cocks his gun. Just in time, he sees who it is)* Matabel!

Matabel passes without seeing or hearing him
and arrives at Thor's Stone

Matabel He must go! — Pixies of Thursley …

Matabel stands poised, then strikes Thor's Stone with the ironstone

(Once from right to left) Save me from him! *(once from left to right)* Save me from him! *(and with the third stroke downward)* Take him away!

Jonas *(Grabbing her from behind)* So, you seek the devil's help to rid yourself of me!

Matabel No!

Jonas Yes! I heard you. "Save me from him. Take him away"

Matabel Jonas, no …

Jonas Take him away. Snap his spine, send a bullet through him, cast him into Pug's mere and drown him — do what you will, only rid me of Bideabout Kink who I swore to love, honour and obey.

Matabel No, Jonas, I did not ask that.

Jonas I heard you.

Matabel Not you

Jonas What? Are these ears not mine?

Matabel I mean, I did not ask to have you taken away.

Jonas Then who? — Listen — I know all now. I trusted you and I believed in you — but Sarah has told me all — how he has been in my house, and how you … *(Pause)*
You cannot answer. You are unable to deny that it was so — you encouraged him into the house …

Matabel No, Jonas, it was you who invited him …

Jonas He would not have come just for me. Little he cared for my society. The picture making was an excuse — you have all been in league against me!

Matabel Who, Jonas?

Jonas Who? Why Sanna Verstage and all. Didn't she ask you to the *Ship* and tell me he was going away? And is he not there still?

Matabel It's false, Jonas.

Jonas False! Who is false but you? *(He grabs her ironstone and hits Thor's Stone with each 'false'):— False* in heart, *false* in word and *false* in deed. Was that daub-paint not in your thoughts when you asked the devil to rid yourself of me?

Matabel That was not what I asked.

Jonas What then? He has not gone away. He has been with you. You knew he was not going. You wanted to be with him. Where is he, this dauber of canvas, now?

At this moment, Iver calls from the distance

Iver Matabel — where are you?

Jonas Oh ho! Here he comes by appointment, to meet you. Here, where you least expected that I would be.

Matabel I came here to escape.

Jonas And pray for my death.

Matabel No, Jonas — to be rid of him.

Jonas Ha! Then I would dearly like to witness this meeting. Summon him here, and let me watch unobserved. If your wish be, as you say, to get rid of him, I will help you in its fulfilment.

Matabel Jonas!

Jonas Come now — if you desired to be rid of him and not me, as you profess, call him. *(Pause)* Answer him. *(Pause)* Say, "I am here".

Matabel *(Shouting to Iver)* I am here.

Iver Where?

Jonas Tell him — by Thor's Stone. Answer him — if you are true, do as I say.

Matabel *(To Iver)* By Thor's Stone.

Jonas rests the gun on Thor's Stone and aims towards Iver

Jonas *(To Matabel)* Stand on one side. Call him again. *(Pause)* Call him again! I will receive him with a dab of lead to his heart. *(Pause)* If false, keep silent — if true, bid him come — to his death, so I can carry out your wish, and rid you of him. If the spirits won't help you, I will.

Matabel Iver, come!

Iver *(Approaching)* You are there!

As Iver appears, Matabel snatches the barrel of the gun and points the muzzle at herself

Matabel *(To Jonas)* Now fire, so all will be well! *(To Iver)* Iver, run! Run! He is here and he will kill you!

Jonas Let go! It's loaded! It'll go off!

Matabel I don't care. Kill me if you will!

There is a fight between them — Iver tries to approach but is slowed by a bog — Jonas finally wrenches the gun away from Matabel, but as he does so it goes off. Matabel screams.

<u>Scene 11</u> In the Punch Bowl

Sarah There's been an accident.

Labourer 1 Down in the Punch Bowl?

Sarah Not down in the Punch Bowl.

Labourer 1 Then where?

Mrs V There's been an accident.

Labourer 2 Here in the bar room?

Mrs V Not here in the bar room.

Labourer 2 Then where?

Chorus

> There's been an accident out on the common there,
> Someone's been given a gunshot-wound injury,
> Someone's been hurt and they may need some surgery,
> Someone is bleeding and needing assistance,
> Someone is offering major resistance,
> But who? —
>
> Someone is trying to sort out the muddle,
> Someone has come out the worst in a struggle,
> Someone is lying face-down in a puddle,
> But who? —

> Someone is coming to call for assistance,
> Someone is coming to call for assistance,
> Someone is coming, yes
> Someone is coming, —
> Someone is coming,
> But who?

At the Ship

Iver A doctor! There is a surgeon staying here at the *Ship* is there
not?

Mrs V Lord, Iver — what's been going on? Who's hurt?

Iver A surgeon, mother! Get the surgeon.

Mrs V Mercy! I'll call him now.

Chorus

> Someone is struggling back to the Punch Bowl,
> Wounded and bleeding, but back to the Punch Bowl,
> On the tracks leading them back to the Punch Bowl,
> But who?

At the Punch Bowl

Jonas Sarah! Where are you?

Sarah Here I be, Jonas. What now?

Jonas I want you at my place. There's been an accident.

Sarah Who to? Not Old Clutch?

Jonas Old Clutch be blowed! It's I that be hurt, terrible bad — in my
arm. Can't you see the blood? Hold up that lantern.

Sarah Where's your wife? Never here when she's wanted, and when
she ain't she's all over the place.

Sarah inspects him — he has been bandaged with Matabel's petticoat

Why, Jonas, you never did this up yourself. There's someone been
at your arm already. Here, this is off Matabel's petticoat — how
came you by that? *(Pause)*
And where's the gun, Jonas?

Jonas The gun? I suppose I've lost it.

Sarah Lost it?

Jonas Somewhere on the common — when I was wounded I hadn't the head to think of nothing else.

Sarah I don't understand your tale a scrap, Jonas. Who used a knife to slit up your sleeve? And how came your arm to be bandaged with this bit of Matabel's dress? *(Pause)*
Jonas, you've seen Matabel and she did this for you. Where is she now?

Jonas Why do you worrit me with questions, woman, when my arm wants attending to?

Sarah I can't do much with that — it needs a doctor. But I'll do nothing more for you till I knows the whole truth. You've seen your wife and there's something passed between you. I can see by your manner that all ain't right. Where is she? *(Pause)*
You haven't been after that deer at all, have you.

Jonas That's a lie. I went out on the moor, and if you will have it all out, it was Matabel who shot me.

Sarah Shot you?

Jonas To stop me killing that painter fellow.

Sarah Then where is she, Jonas? I will know all.

Jonas Then know it. She was helping me along home when her foot slipped and she fell into the bog. I had but one arm and I were stiff with pain — what could I do?

Sarah Her in the bog? — why didn't you say that at once?

Jonas Aren't I hurt terrible bad? Ain't I got a broken arm or something like it?

Sarah Jonas, where did you leave her?

Jonas Right along between here and Thor's Stone — by an old twisted scotch pine with magpies' nests in it. She may have crawled out, or she may be still lying there. How should I know in my condition?

Sarah What have you done? You've killed her, haven't you. I said you should never have married her as was marked with the gibbet — now we'll have another gibbet down here, for us to swing on.

They hear voices approaching

Jonas It's the constables! Save me, Sally! Hide me.

He hides as Iver and the surgeon arrive

Sarah *(To Jonas)* It's that Master Iver, with another man.

Jonas The constable!

Sarah Don't be a fool — come out, or you'll make them suspect you!

Jonas *(Coming out)* Your servants, gentlemen.

Iver I have brought you a surgeon, Jonas.

Jonas You be a doctor, sir? I've met with an accident, sir — my gun went off and …

Doctor *(Inspecting Jonas)* I must have hot water. Can somebody …

Sarah I'll get that for you, sir.

Doctor Thank you.

Iver Where is your wife, Jonas?

Jonas Her? She lagged behind.

Iver That's not possible — she was helping you home.

Jonas I didn't need assistance. *(The surgeon works on him)* Ouch!

Iver She should be here. Where is Matabel?

Jonas It's none of your business where she be.

Sarah He says they were coming home together, like loving man and wife, when she chanced to slip and fell in the bog — and what with Jonas having his arm so bad …

Iver *(To Jonas)* You left her lying in the bog?

Jonas You don't suppose I threw her in? Not with my arm …

Iver Bideabout, I will have a proper explanation from you, or I will fetch the constable. Tell me, where is Matabel?

Jonas Some place where you can't get at her …

Iver I warn you, if you have harmed her …

Jonas Where she's safe from you …

Iver Jonas!

Jonas Where you won't see her again — ever.

Matabel enters, dishevelled and holding the gun, aimed at Jonas

Matabel?

Iver Matabel, you're safe!

Matabel And how is your injury, Jonas?

Iver We were told you had fallen in the bog.

Matabel *(Putting the gun down)* Yes, I fell. But I held onto his gun, and it kept me from sinking.

Iver But how …

Matabel *(Dismissing Iver)* And now, I must attend to my husband.

> Attend to my husband,
> Make sense of my vows —
> Till death do us part.

<u>Scene 12</u> **The Birth**

Mrs V So you're finally leaving.

Iver For Guildford, yes mother.

Mrs V And Matabel?

Iver Seems to have found her devotion to duty.

Mrs V What happened, that night on the common?

Iver Well, I didn't shoot him — that's all I can tell you.

Sarah So, you shot my brother.

Matabel Is that what he said?

Sarah Aye, those were his words, but …

Matabel Then best not discuss it.

Sarah That night on the common, he left you for dead.

Matabel I don't really remember. Don't really

M & Mrs V *(together)* remember —

Mrs V that night you ran out — what was all the commotion?

Matabel My husband had need of me.

Mrs V Out on the common?

Matabel Oh, mother, I fell — I forget all the details.

Mrs V If I can't be trusted …

Matabel I'd trust you with anything … but, please, not that.

Mrs V Well then, let's change the subject. I've brought you a present.
A cookery book that was given to me — I'd not give it to anyone.

Matabel Mother, how kind!

Mrs V They're peculiar creatures are men, but you'll find if you keep
them well fed they'll be happy most times. How are things now,
between you?

Matabel I wouldn't say easy — but look, there's a secret I wanted to
share with you. *(She whispers in Mrs Verstage's ear)* No-one else
knows it.

Mrs V That's famous! That's wonderful — just as it ought to be!
Have you told Jonas yet? *(Matabel shakes her head)* He'll be
delighted — there's nothing like that to make a home homely.

Jonas I know who you're thinking of.

Matabel Thinking of?

Jonas You with a faraway look in your eye. It's that dauber of paints
again!

Matabel Jonas, how can you …

Jonas *(Mimics)* "How can you"? Deny it, if you have the nerve to!
Your guilt keeps you silent.

Matabel I once swore to love you — and Heaven can answer for all
my endeavours, to force love to grow where it doesn't grow
naturally. Jonas, it only takes some small return on your part, and
we'd find common ground — we could meet and be happy. But no,
you mistrust me.

Jonas Mistrust you, I do. That doctor — you know that he gave me
some medicine, something to ease the distress in my shoulder —
laudanum, it was — but I couldn't take it — no, I had to suffer, and

why? Because I couldn't trust you to pour me the measure. You'd double the dose and be glad to be rid of me.

Matabel Jonas, I'd never …

Jonas So it's locked in the cupboard, and I've got the key — and that's where it stays till the day I've the strength to remove it.

Chorus

As weeks turned to months, and spring turned to summer,
Jonas made plans, soon to come to a head;
While back in the *Ship*, disease struck a blow
and old Sanna Verstage was taken to bed.

And just before the scythe cut the first green swarth of hay,
(We hear the sound of a baby crying)
Matabel became a mother.

<u>Scene 13</u> The Bequest

Mrs Verstage is ill in bed — Matabel is with her

Mrs V My dear Matabel, it's no use you wishing and hoping. Wishing and hoping never made puff paste without lard. I haven't got in me one thing which would raise me up again. But there, no more about me — show me the young broom-squire.

Matabel hands her the baby — [Baring-Gould says that the 'usual scene incident upon the exhibition of a babe' ensues]

Mrs V And how do you and your husband stand to each other now.

Matabel I'd rather you didn't ask.

Mrs V That tells me all. I'd had hopes that this little lad would have made it all right between you, but I see plain that he has not.

Matabel Mother …

Mrs V Listen to me. Now I stand with two feet on the brink of my grave, I see matters in a very different light from what I did before. I can see now I did wrong in pushing you to take Bideabout. I've fretted a good deal over it, but the thing is done now and cannot be undone.

Matabel You need say no more — I have my baby now, and I am happy.

Mrs V God has given you that, but I have given you nothing — nothing to make amends for the spoiling of your life. And give you something I must. So my plan is this — I have saved some money which was intended for Iver, but he doesn't need it greatly. I intend to leave you a hundred and fifty pounds.

Matabel Mother, I pray you do nothing of the kind.

Mrs V I must do it, Matabel, to ease my mind.

Matabel It will make me miserable.

Mrs V Why so? I intend this money to be your very own — it shall be yours, and yours only.

Matabel Mother, it will only make matters worse. Jonas does not hold with us having separate purses. If you must leave the money, may it be left to the baby instead of me?

Mrs V Certainly, if you like it — but there must be someone to look after it for him till he comes of age. I'll have to think of a suitable trustee, so the little man shall have a hundred and fifty pounds as a stand-by in case his father fools away his own money, which in my opinion is most likely. What has Jonas done with all the money he's saved?

Matabel It's still in the Bank, as far as I know.

Mrs V He's ever picking up money, but it never seems to do him a scrap of good.

<u>Scene 14</u> The Baptism Party in the Punch Bowl

The party sit at a table spread with food — Jonas & Matabel, Giles & Betsy Cheel, Tom & Sarah Rocliffe, the Boxalls. Giles Cheel rises.

Giles Cheel Ladies and gentlemen, neighbours all — I suppose on such an occasion as this, and after such a feed to celebrate the Christening of Jonas's new son, it's the duty of one of us to make a speech. And as I'm the oldest and most respected of the broom-squires of the Bowl, I think it proves as I should express the general feeling of satisfaction we all have.
That there rabbit pie might have been proud to call itself hare. The current wine was comforting, especially to such as myself who has a touch of a chill below the ribs, and it helps the digestion. There be some new-fangled notions coming up about teetotalling. I don't hold with them. The world was once drowned with water, and I don't see why we should have Noah's Floods in our innards.

Betsy Cheel Sit down, Gilly Cheel — you're rambling from the point.

Giles Cheel You let go, Betsy — I'm rambling up to it.

Betsy Cheel Sit down, they've had enough of you.

Giles Cheel They've hardly had a taste.

Betsy Cheel Everyone be laughing at you.

Giles Cheel I'm just about bringing tears into their eyes.

Betsy Cheel If you go on, I'll clap my hand over your mouth

Giles Cheel And I'll punch your head.

Jonas rises

Jonas Neighbours and friends all. Very obliged for the compliment, but don't think it's all about a baby. Nothing of the kind. It's because I wanted you all to be together while I make an announcement which will be pleasant hearing to some parties, and astonishing to all.

Sarah *(To her neighbours)* Don't like the sound of this. Jonas is looking altogether too happy for my liking.

Jonas I ain't going to detain you very long, for what I have to say might be packed in a nutshell and carried away in the stomach of a tomtit.

You all of you know, good friends, as how my brother-in-law Tom Rocliffe once made a fool of himself through marrying a Countess Charlotte — who turned out not to be a countess after all, but an impostor who ran off with all his money. And how his farm got mortgaged because of it, and then the lawyers charged up his debt even more, so their family have led a struggling life since just to keep their heads above water. Well, I've got all their mortgages and debts into my hands now.

Sarah Jonas!

Jonas No, sister, I don't intend to give them up like you're hoping. I'm keeping hold of them, and I ain't going to stand no shilly-shallying about the payments when due — you can be sure of that. And what's more, I won't stand no nonsense from you — I expect you to be my very humble servants from now on, or I'll sell you up!

He turns to the Cheels

And I've something to say to Gilly Cheel. I ain't going to have the Punch Bowl made a devil's cauldron with his constant quarrelling.

Betsy Cheel Hear, hear.

Jonas And unless he lives peaceable, and don't trouble me with his noise and she with her caterwauling …

Giles Cheel *(To Betsy)* That's for you!

Jonas … I'll turn them both out, for I've been getting his papers into my hands too.

He turns to the Boxalls

And as to the Boxalls — if their time hasn't come yet, it's coming. Now I hope, neighbours and friends all, you've enjoyed the dessert.

Sarah *(Flinging an envelope at Jonas)* You can take that, then. I don't want to be burdened with nothing of yours. It's a letter as has been lying around at the post for you — Mrs Chivers gave it me. Wish I was rid of everything between us as I be of that there letter now.

Jonas carelessly opens the letter, then sits suddenly as he reads it

Jonas The Wealden Bank — it's gone broke. I'm a ruined man!

Stunned silence, then laughter from the others as they exit.

*** Interval ***

During which 7 members of the audience are selected
to act as Jurymen in Scene 22

<u>Scene 15</u> The Trustee

Sarah My brother Jonas, the only man in the Punch Bowl to trust his money to a Bank — and why? — because he didn't trust us.

Jonas You'd have stolen it from me while I were away — I know you would.

Sarah So now the Bank's closed down and he's lost it all.

Jonas Worse, I'm in debt. Still have to pay that attorney for his work.

Sarah Him and that attorney, they were plotting to buy us out …

Jonas … and for nothing.

Sarah They never managed to do it — not before the Bank closed. So who's laughing now? Ha ha!

Jonas Family!

Sarah Well you needn't look this way. You married outside the Bowl, Jonas Kink, and it's outside the Bowl you must now go for help.

Jonas If I don't find a hundred and fifty pounds in short order, my own house is forfeit.

Simon Ah, Bideabout, been looking for you.

Jonas Why's that?

Simon You heard about Sanna.

Jonas What of her?

Simon She's gone.

Jonas Gone? Where to?

Simon That's not for me to say. I s'pose it's ordained. And her so hearty only a month ago.

Jonas Dead, you mean?

Simon We knew it must come, but nobody thought it would come so sudden.

Jonas You said you were looking for me.

Simon There's a message for Matabel from Sanna, 'fore she went. You'll let her know?

Jonas What message is that?

Simon About the bequest. The money she'd promised.

Jonas Money you say? How much money?

Simon A hundred and fifty pounds — you'll take the message, will you? Only we're that tied up at the *Ship* …

Jonas A hundred and fifty pounds? Oh aye, I'll take it.

Simon The message. I can't give you the money, of course.

Jonas Can't? Why ever not. It's for Matabel you say, and we're as one.

Simon Oh no, it's not for Matabel — it's for the baby.

Jonas It's all the same — I'm its father, and I'll take care of the money.

Simon But I can't give it you.

Jonas Haven't you got it?

Simon Oh, I've got it alright — but the child won't be old enough to enjoy it for many years.

Jonas But in the meantime …

Simon She were a wonderful shrewd woman, were Sanna. She wouldn't make me a trustee for the money — said I was too old and foolish, to use her very words. So she put it all in the hands of Iver, to hold for the little chap.

Jonas Iver — trustee for my child?

Simon Aye — and why not?

Jonas Then I shall have words with Master Iver.

Simon He's in Guildford.

Jonas I know he's in Guildford — and it's to Guildford that I'm a'going!

<u>Scene 16</u> Markham visits Matabel

Markham arrives; Matabel is tending the baby

Markham I have come to see Mr Kink — this is his house I believe?

Matabel Yes sir, but he's not presently at home.

Markham Will he be long absent?

Matabel I'm afraid I don't know. Will you take a chair?

Markham I want to do some fishing, and Mr Kink was kind enough to attend me on a shoot during the winter. Excuse me, but are you his sister or his wife?

Matabel His wife, sir.

Markham You are very young … and uncommonly pretty. Where the deuce did the broomsquire pick you up?

Matabel Can I give a message to my husband?

Markham A message? You can tell him he's a lucky dog. I had no idea such a pearl lay at the bottom of the Punch Bowl. And that is your baby?

Matabel It is, sir.

Markham It looks as if it were for another world, not this one.

Matabel You are not a doctor, are you?

Markham Oh dear no! — a barrister.

Matabel Then you do not know. The child is very well, but young.

Markham I want Kink to accompany me on one of the ponds hereabouts. There must be plenty of fish in these sheets of water.

Matabel I believe there are, sir. Perhaps as Jonas is away Samuel Rocliffe can help you — he is my husband's nephew, in the cottage a little further down.

Markham Hang me, but I do not care to leave!

Matabel Sir, I …

Markham My pretty hostess, if I ever begrudged a man anything in my life, I begrudge Jonas Kink his wife. Come and tell me when you find him intolerable, and see if I cannot provide some professional help to rid you of such a curmudgeon.

Matabel I hardly think that likely, sir.

Markham Who knows? The time may come! My name is Markham — good day to you.

<u>Scene 17</u> Jonas visits Iver in Guildford

Jonas arrives at Iver's Guildford studio – there is a picture of Matabel on display. Iver has brush in one hand mahlstick in the other (p.76)

Jonas *(Offering his hand)* Master Iver, good day to you.

Iver makes pretence of looking for somewhere to put his brushes down – does not shake hands

(Jonas drops his hand) Let bygones be bygones. Fine picture that; very like my wife. How much have you sold it for?

Iver It's not for sale.

Jonas Why's that?

Iver Because it's a good sample of my ability which I can show to customers — and because it reminds me of an old friend.

Jonas Old friend! She's got a baby now — but I suppose you know that.

Iver Did you come all the way from the Punch Bowl just to see the painting?

Jonas No I didn't. I've come, civil and neighbour-like, to see you — on business.

Iver What business is that?

Jonas You're a trustee, I hear, for my child.

Iver To be sure, I am. The money is for your little one when he has come of age.

Jonas Well, I need it now.

Iver But you cannot have it.

Jonas See here, Master Iver Verstage, you never ought to have been made trustee — it's so much as putting a slight and an insult on me. If that child be mine, then I'm the one should have the trust.

Iver It's not a question of what should be — I didn't seek to be the trustee — it was an idea on the part of my dear mother. She has done it, and there it is — neither you nor I can alter that.

Jonas He may never come of age.

Iver That we cannot predict.

Jonas Aren't you bound to spend it on the child?

Iver I am bound to preserve it whole and intact for him.

Jonas But can you not see that, for the child's sake, I need the money now?

Iver That is possible, but my hands are tied.

Jonas You will not give it to me.

Iver I cannot.

Jonas I don't believe you. You do this to spite me.

Iver Not at all, Bideabout. I wish the child and its mother well, and of course you, but I cannot break a trust.

Jonas You will not.

Iver If no other word will suit you, so be it — I will not.

Jonas I shouldn't be surprised if it's you who's been at the bottom of all this. You want to buy me up and buy me out so that you and Matabel can have the place to yourselves. Well, it'll never be. I'm to be reckoned with, I can assure you of that. I'll find the means to keep my property from you, and my wife too. *(He starts beating and tearing the picture of Matabel)* Not even her picture shall you have. I wish it were her I was slashing and breaking to pieces, and it may come to that in the end — for out of my power and into your hands she will never go!

<u>Scene 18</u> Matabel takes the baby to see Sarah

Sarah I tell you what I think — someone has cast an evil eye on this child. See that little vein there? It's the colour of them whortleberries — that's a sure sign someone bears the poor creature no love.

Matabel But who has done it?

Sarah That's not for me to say. It's someone who doesn't love the babe, that's certain.

Matabel What can I do for him?

Sarah There's nothing. Misfortune and wasting away will be his lot, unless …

Matabel Unless what?

Sarah They do say, if you was to take it to Thor's stone and carry it thrice round, way of the sun, you might cast off the ill wish. But I can't say — I've never tried it.

Matabel The weather's too cold for that, and he's too ill. My poor darling.

<u>Scene 19</u> Jonas sees Barelegs the attorney

Barelegs Ah, come in Mr Kink.

Jonas You look at me, Mr Barelegs, like my horse does when he wants his feed of corn.

Barelegs And no doubt he deserves it.

Jonas He thinks he does, but he don't.

Barelegs But no doubt he gets his feed.

Jonas He gets it when I choose to give it, not when he glowers at me.

Barelegs I dare say if he has served you well he expects to be paid for it.

Jonas He may well expect.

Barelegs And if he does not receive his feed, does he not kick and bite?

Jonas He tried that once, but he won't try it again. I have my ways with him.

Barelegs Well, Mr Kink, you haven't come here to ask for my assistance with your horse.

Jonas No, that's gospel. It's against Iver Verstage, that painter chap at Guildford.

Barelegs What has he been doing?

Jonas Nothing — that's just it. He's been made trustee for my child, and I want the money out.

Barelegs Out of his pocket and into yours.

Jonas Exactly.

Barelegs I can't help you. You can't touch the sum until your son comes of age.

Jonas That's twenty-one years from now!

Barelegs I'm very sorry, but that bequest is beyond your reach so long as the child lives.

Jonas What's that you say?

Barelegs I say that unless the poor creature should die, you cannot finger the money.

Jonas And if it dies, would it be mine?

Barelegs Of course it would. But by no other means can you get it. And, please heaven, the child will grow to be a strong man and outlive you.

Jonas Yes, but it's wonderful weakly …

Barelegs And now may we consider my fee? I think we must have all clear an straight between us, and that soon. Here is my account. *(Hands him a paper)* You will remember that, acting on your instructions, I advanced money in certain transactions that have broken down through the unfortunate failure of the Wealden Bank…

Jonas A hundred and fifty pounds.

Barelegs I will not be hard on you, but of course you do not expect me to make you a present of my money and my professional service.

Jonas That's the sum that Iver Verstage holds, of my money.

Barelegs Let us not reopen that wound, Mr Kink. I daresay that among your neighbours you may be able to borrow sufficient.

Jonas Can't borrow off them — I've offended them all.

Barelegs Then have you no other friends to whom you may apply?

Jonas No, not one.

Barelegs Then there must be some fault in you. A man who goes through life without making friends is not one who will leave a gap when he passes out of the world. I shall expect my money. I shall not press you at once, but, like your horse, I shall want my feed of oats.

Jonas Then I see no other way of getting the money than …

Barelegs Than what?

Jonas That's my business.

Scene 20 Back at the Punch Bowl

Sarah Somebody bears the poor creature no love.

Matabel Somebody wishes my treasure no joy.

Sarah That little vein, purple like hurts on the common,
A sure sign that somebody's troubled the boy.

Jonas I got a bottle of medicine for the child while I were in Godalming.

Matabel Medicine?

Jonas From the doctor.

Matabel Did you tell him exactly what ailed the baby?

Jonas I reckon I did. Cost me half a crown.

Matabel Then let me have the bottle …

Jonas Don't be in such a wonderful hurry. I've other things to do than get that out yet. How is the child?

Matabel A little better, I think.

Jonas *(Scowling)* Better?

Matabel Oh Jonas! Does it mean nothing to you that the baby is ill? You surely don't want him to die?

Jonas What makes you say that?

Matabel Oh, nothing. Only you don't seem to care a bit about him.

Jonas But he's better, you say?

Matabel I really do think so.

Jonas Then, I'd best get on with things.

We see Jonas tampering with the medicine during the next lines …

Sarah Somebody bears the poor creature no love.

Matabel But Jonas has brought back a cure for the boy.

Sarah Somebody wishes him out of this world,
        And will turn things around for themselves to enjoy.

Jonas Here's your medicine. Now the child can have it.

Matabel Perhaps, as he's better, I needn't give it to him now.

Jonas That's just like your ways! First I get no rest till I promise to go to the doctor, then when I've put myself out to go, and bring back a bottle as has cost me half a crown, you won't have it.

Matabel But it's only because …

Jonas You do it to spite me. The child is ill. The doctor said as this would put him to rights and get him to sleep, and give us all some rest. Give him the medicine. *(Moves away)*

Matabel Perhaps I should. *(She looks at the bottle)* But this looks strange — it seems to be unmixed — as if someone has added one medicine on top of another. *(She opens the bottle to sniff)*

Sarah Somebody bears the poor creature no love,
　　　Someone has gone to the safe with a key,
　　　Taken the bottle, removed half the contents,
　　　And …

Jonas *(Aside)* Filled it with laudanum given to me.

Matabel *(Recognising the smell)* No! Jonas, no! Not one drop shall
　　he have! *(She throws the bottle away)* My babe, my poor babe —
　　no-one in the world loves you but me. No-one.

Jonas *(Entering)* Have you given the child the medicine?

Matabel Not all.

Jonas Of course, not all.

Matabel Will it make my baby sleep?

Jonas Oh, sleep — sleep! Yes, we shall have rest for one night — for
　　many, I trust. Oh yes, don't doubt it — it will make the brat sleep.
　　(Exits)

<u>Scene 21</u> Matabel on the run

Chorus And now in the dark of a cold winter's night,
　　　When the mists in the Bowl cheat the moon of her light,
　　　Matabel places the babe in its bed
　　　And gets herself rested — but only half-settled.
　　　Then secretly, silently, Jonas appears.
　　　By the rush-candle light, we see him come near
　　　to the cot where the babe rests, a little too healthy.
　　　He takes up its pillow and, slowly and stealthily,
　　　lowers it firm on the little chap's head.
　　　But Matabel stirs, and before the brat's dead
　　　she's across to the crib, between father and son,
　　　and, with baby clasped tightly, she turns and she runs

from the house of her nightmares to raise the alarm.
But who will protect her?

Sarah Where be you a'going at this time of the morning, dressed like that? — and with the child too.

Matabel I can't tell you.

Sarah But I will know.

Matabel I'm never coming back here again.

Sarah Oh, kicked you out, has he?

Matabel I'm running away.

Sarah And where to?

Matabel I don't know. *(Moves away)*

Sarah *(After her)* But I do! You'll be away after that Iver Verstage, I've no doubt.

Matabel moves to the Ship, and meets Simon

Simon Matabel! Glad to see you. What brings you here so early in the day?

Matabel Father, I can't tell you everything, but I've left Bideabout. I can't stay with him any longer. Will you take me in at the *Ship*?

Simon Well, I'll have to consult with Molly about that.

Matabel Molly?

Simon Now poor Sanna's gone, Molly's taken on the management. I'll go and ask her.

Matabel But father …

Simon I can't say 'yes' without her say so now.

Matabel And she'll say my father lies in Thursley churchyard — I'm still a Charity Girl to her — she'll not let me in.

Simon It's not my wish.

Matabel I'll trouble you no further, dear father. Who is the Guardian of the Poor now?

Simon That'll be Timothy Puttenham, the wheelwright.

Matabel Then the Charity Girl will have to beg for charity there.

Puttenham You? Want to live in the Poor House? What is the sense of this? You have a home in the Punch Bowl.

Matabel I have left it.

Puttenham Then you must return to it again.

Matabel I cannot.

Puttenham My good girl, this is rank nonsense. The Poor House is not for such as you.

Matabel I need its shelter. I have no home.

Puttenham Are you gone off your head?

Matabel No, sir. My mind is sound, but I will never return to the Punch Bowl again. I can't and I won't, ever.

Puttenham It is not 'cannot' and 'will not' — it is a case of 'must'. That is your home. Now, if you would like to ask my old woman for some breakfast, I'll send my apprentice to bid Jonas come and fetch you home.

Matabel If Jonas comes, I will run away.

Puttenham But where? Where can you go except back to your husband's house? For God's sake! Don't say you're going to Guildford, to that Iver Verstage.

Matabel I would rather throw myself into one of the hammer ponds than do that.

She moves away

Markham Why, it is the Squiress again. And what brings you out on the moor here?

Matabel I have run away from the Punch Bowl.

Markham What! Fallen out with the Broomsquire?

Matabel He's made it impossible for me.

Markham So where are you going?

Matabel I have no idea.

Markham Now see here, I am a lawyer. Tell me all, and I daresay I can help you.

Matabel There's not much to tell. Things have happened, and I'd go anywhere and do anything rather than go back

Markham Has he been beating you?

Matabel Oh no, not that. There are worse things to bear than a stick.

Markham Oh ho! He has been casting his eye about and has lost his leathery heart to some other wench. Have I hit it? It is jealousy at the bottom of it.

Matabel No, you do not understand me. Jonas has not sunk so low as that.

Markham He is a poor, sordid creature, not worthy of you. You are a jewel. But come. A lawyer is a confessor. Open your heart to me and see if the law, or I myself, cannot assist you. Are you seeking a home and protector?

Matabel I want to earn a living somewhere.

Markham And a pretty young thing like you cannot fail to make her way. Come! I have offered you my aid. *(He puts his arms round her and attempts to snatch a kiss)*

Matabel No! So this is the friend and protector you'd be. I trust you with my troubles, and you take advantage. Leave me alone!

She moves away

Sarah There's all the Punch Bowl turned out, some running one way and some the other, all looking for Matabel. Some says she's off her head, some thinks she's drowned herself and the child. And there's Jonas storming around, and my Thomas gone with him. But I came this way, and here you are. How's the child?

Matabel He is well, now we are out of the Punch Bowl.

Sarah You'll have to go back when Jonas fetches you.

Matabel Never!

Sarah He'll get the constable to force you home if he has to. The law of the land is against you.

Matabel I will not go back.

Sarah Don't know where he is right now. I've a notion he's prowling about the common thinking you may have gone back to Thor's Stone. But come he will, and he'll take you and the baby, and you may squeal and scratch as you like, but go back with him you must.

Matabel I'm as strong as he is — stronger, for I will fight for my
child. I will kill him rather than let him take my baby from me.

Sarah There's folks as say you tried to do for him once before, with
the gun.

Matabel Let him try! I will do it again. I will …

Sarah Mercy, you're possessed! I'll have no more to do with this.
(She moves off)

Matabel Yes — possessed with a mother's love. He will not so much
as touch the baby, ever — or if he should try …

Suddenly, Jonas is before her

Jonas So, I have found you at last!

Matabel Yes, you have found me.

Jonas Do you know what you have done? Made me a derision and
talk to all Thursley, and in every pot house.

Matabel I have not done this — it is your doing.

Jonas Isn't it enough that I've lost all my money? Now I must have
scandal in my own home as well. You will come back with me at
once.

Matabel I will not go with you.

Jonas You are mad. You must be put under restraint.

Matabel I'd rather go to the madhouse than back to the Punch Bowl.

Jonas You shall be forced to return.

Matabel How?

Jonas I will have you tied up. I'll swear you're crazed. I'll lock you
up and beat you till you learn to obey and behave as I would have
you.

Matabel Jonas, this is idle talk. Never, never will I go back with you.

Jonas Never!

Matabel has a piece of ironstone in her hand

Matabel You may threaten, but threats do not move me. I can defend
myself.

Jonas *(Scoffing)* With a small stone?

Matabel Yes, if needs be with a stone. But I have better protection than that.

Jonas Indeed? Let me hear of it.

Matabel I shall appeal to the law.

Jonas The law? It's the law that will send you back to me.

Matabel It is the law which will protect me from you.

Jonas I'd like to learn how.

Matabel I've only to go before a magistrate and tell how you tried to poison your own child — and how when that failed you tried to smother him. And, Jonas …

> *Matabel steps forward raising the stone, and Jonas steps back*

… with the like of this stone you tried to kill me on the common. You are a would-be murderer of both your wife and your child — and I am free of you!

Matabel takes another step forward — Jonas disappears with a scream into a hole

Chorus

> Some say he tripped — and some say she pushed him,
> No-one could swear to it, no-one was near enough.
> How Jonas fell down the lime kiln that day,
> Through the earth into the lime kiln that day,
> Fell to his death in lime kiln that day,
> Nobody knew — but most had opinions.

The Judge is already in the court room

Judge

> The law gives protection to those seeking justice,
> The law gives protection to those who've been wronged,
> The law is an instrument blind in its favours
> 'twixt taking and giving, 'twixt dead and the living —
> And Matabel came to be judged …

<u>Scene 22</u> The Trial

Judge I call on the counsel for the prosecution to sum up in this case.

Markham M'lord, members of the Jury. This case is a peculiarly painful one for me. For in it, we see exhibited the blackest ingratitude in one who owed, I might say, everything to the deceased. As the court has heard, the accused was brought up in a small wayside tavern where she served in the capacity of barmaid, giving drink to the low fellows who frequented the public house — and I need hardly say that such a bringing up must necessarily kill all the modesty, morality, self-respect and common decency out of a young girl's mind.

From this situation, she was rescued by Jonas Kink, a substantial farmer, who, we might say, lifted the unfortunate creature from the gutter. He gave her his name, he gave her a home, and he treated her with uniform kindness. You have heard no evidence, members of the Jury, that he ever maltreated her — on the contrary, the prisoner herself has said that he has never struck her with a stick.

But, I ask you to consider, what husband would endure that the young wife who was so indebted to him for everything, should resume her light and reprehensible conduct after he had made her his own?

No doubt whatever, that the prisoner at the bar felt the monotony of a farmhouse irksome after the lively experience in a public house. No doubt she missed the society of topers and their tipsy familiarities. But was that reason enough to kill her husband?

I believe I have been able to show that this murder was planned, that the prisoner provided herself with the implement and, with the deliberate intention to free herself, waited to catch her husband alone where she believed she would be unobserved, and knocked him into a disused lime kiln. A woman who could do this is not one who should be suffered to live; she is a scandal to her sex; she dishonours humanity; she cannot be allowed to run free.

I will lose no more words, but demand a sentence of guilty against Mehetabel Kink.

Judge I now call upon the counsel for the defence.

Counsel for the defence begins,
but our attention switches to the public gallery

Labourer 1 *(To his neighbour)* Here, ain't that Iver Verstage with the jury?

Labourer 2 Well, I'm blessed if it ain't. How come he's managed to get himself in there.

Labourer 1 Lord knows. That ain't legal, is it? Not if he knows her.

Labourer 2 I suppose no-one here knows that he does.

Labourer 1 There's Sarah Rocliffe and her Thomas — they ought to say something about it.

Labourer 2 Them? They're too thick to know what day of the week it is.

Counsel for Defence … so I entreat you, members of the Jury, not to be led away by appearances, but to weigh the evidence you have heard carefully in you own minds, and to pronounce as your verdict — not guilty.

Judge The Jury will now retire …

In the Jury Room[†]

Iver So, my fellow Jury members, what do you make of that? Do we pronounce her 'guilty' or 'not guilty'?

Juryman 1 I say hang her. It won't do to let wives think they can play old Harry with their husbands and massacre them with impunity. I say guilty. Hang her.

Juryman 2 If she weren't so good-looking, I'd say let her off. But my wife's in court, and it's as much as my domestic bliss is worth, gentlemen, to say not guilty. So for peace and quiet, I say guilty. Hang her.

[†] Selected members of the audience are here invited to come forward and act as Jurymen

Juryman 3 I don't know as I care particularly, but as far as I'm concerned it's better to hang her even if she's innocent. It's setting a good example to women. I say guilty. Hang her.

Juryman 4 I wouldn't want to differ from anyone. I'd rather you passed me over now and ask the rest. I'll just fall in with the general decision.

Juryman 5 I'm rather hard of hearing and didn't catch all the evidence — and I'd had a bad night and I closed my eyes now and then — so I'm not well up on the case. But I say guilty. Hang her.

Iver Well I say, emphatically, not guilty. The whole thing is rank nonsense. How could a woman with a baby in her arms knock a man down? You try it.

No, I tell you, the man was a curmudgeon. He misused her. He was in debt, he wanted money, and the child had just been left a fortune …

Juryman 1 How do you know that? It didn't come out in court.

Iver Perhaps you shut your ears as this gentleman did his eyes. The fellow wanted money, and Matabel — I mean, the prisoner at the bar — thought, rightly or wrongly, that he wanted to kill the child for it.

Juryman 1 But that was never in the evidence.

Iver Was it not? Then so much the worse for the case. It wasn't properly got up. But I'll tell you what, gents — if you and me can't agree, then the Jury will be dismissed and we will look like a parcel of noodles to our friends. So what do you think?

Juryman 6 I'd like to know what the cost of an execution to the ratepayers is — must be well over a hundred pounds — that'll mean another farthing stuck on the rates. Not guilty. Let her go.

Juryman 7 And I am averse to capital punishment — I wrote a little tract on the subject if any of you are interested *(offers them around)* so I must positively say 'not guilty'.

Iver So, so far four say guilty and three say not guilty, with one abstention. And how about the rest of you?

Back in court

Judge Have you, members of the Jury, reached a unanimous decision?

Iver We have.

Judge And do you find the prisoner guilty or not guilty?

Iver Not guilty.

Matabel *(Curtseying to the Judge)* Then please, sir, may I return to my baby now?

As the court empties

Sarah Not guilty? She's as guilty as the day is long. I may not have had a good word to say about my brother while he was alive — but family's family and this ain't justice. *(Towards Matabel)* You wait till you try and come back to the Punch Bowl — don't think you'll be welcome, you murderer.

Sarah berating Matabel
(Pru Harrold and Isabelle Glinn)
Rural Life Centre, Tilford, June 2013

<u>Scene 23</u> At the Ship Inn

Iver Was it not a piece of rare good luck that I was stuck on the jury? But I would still like to know the truth about what happened at the old kiln.

Matabel There's nothing to tell — the words I spoke made Jonas spring back. Neither he nor I knew of the open pit behind.

Iver But you laughed.

Matabel Oh Iver, I don't know what I did. I was frightened out of my wits. There are times when a laugh comes because tears won't break out.

Iver That's like enough. So his house is now yours.

Matabel I'm not going to the Punch Bowl ever again.

Iver But you must — it's your home. You have no other.

Matabel It's no home to me.

Iver So, where …?

Matabel Now you're coming back to live at the *Ship*, I thought — may I not stay and be a servant here?

Iver Here? But Mattie, that would never do.

Matabel Why not?

Iver A number of reasons. In the first place, there's been chatter about my being on the jury, and some folk say we found you not guilty just because I … and I'm not saying there isn't some truth in that. But there is more. I have got engaged to Polly Colpus.

Matabel Engaged!

Iver You see, she's the only child of James Colpus, and his land adjoins ours, and when the old man dies …

Matabel But she has a moustache!

Iver *(a pause)* I won't hurry you, not for another ten minutes or so, but under the circumstances … I doubt if I'm acting sensibly letting you in the house.

Matabel Once the door to the *Ship* was open to all but you, Iver —
now it's open to all but me.

Iver Be reasonable, Matabel. You have a home in the Punch Bowl …

Matabel I have no home — no home at all. It seems I've been spared
the gallows only to become a wanderer again.

Thor's Stone on Thursley Common
photographed in the early 20th century

<u>Scene 24</u> To Thor's Stone again

Sarah Now <u>he's</u> dead and gone, and <u>she's</u> not returning,
I reckon old Jonas's place is our own.

Matabel Never the Punch Bowl, not if they dragged me there,
Even though Jonas has gone, there's the rest of them,
Scowling and squabbling , brawling and bickering,
Couldn't live <u>there</u> with them, *(to baby)* could we my darling.

Sarah Thought he'd be better'n us, wedding a gallows girl,
Marrying charity outside the Punch Bowl —
Lawd, what a lesson! And didn't he pay for it.

Matabel Could we my darling? My own sweet … my darling?
How cold you are — cold you are. Out on the common,
the common at Pudmore,
by Thor's stone at night-time, where … accidents happen,
and … pixies are gathering —
Why are you gathering? Where are you coming from?
What are you coming for? <u>Who</u> are you coming for?
Not for my precious! Not for my baby!
Take me instead, not …

Sarah … And didn't he pay for it.
A hornet lived in a hollow tree,
A proper spiteful twoad were he,
And he said as married he'd happy be,
But all the folks jeered and laughed at he!

And even his son ain't survived to be free.

They do say as how she — that is, his wife, the gallows girl — she
finally got lodgings with the old school governess at Thursley —
but, I neither know nor care.

<u>Scene 25</u> Finale

We hear a school bell ringing offstage

Mrs V In the fullness of time, the old schoolma'am of Thursley
sickened and died and was gathered to dust.

Simon Matabel Kink, the Broomsquire's young widow,
took over the running …

Sarah … took over the running …

Simon   … became the new schoolma'am …

Matabel *(Entering with bell)* … and taught what should be taught as a
matter of course:
to love and fear God;
that C A T spells cat and D O G spells dog;
and that two and two makes four, and three times four makes
twelve.

Simon … Matabel Kink, the old Broomsquire's widow …

Mrs V … who once was Mehetabel, found in the Punch Bowl …

Iver … marked with the gallows …

Jonas … saved from a hanging.

Sarah Some say he tripped …

Jonas …and some say she pushed him …

Simon & Iver … who knows …

Mrs V, Jonas & Sarah … who can tell?

All Only she!

*The cast assemble, take their bows to all sides, and invite the audience
to join them in a 'Grand Circle Dance' to end the show*

Jonas confronts Iver in his artist's studio
Rural Life Centre, Tilford, September 2000

Audience joining in the Grand Circle Dance
Rural Life Centre, Tilford, June 2013

Director's Notes

A substantial proportion of the script is written in 'rhythmic' form — sometimes this is obvious (as in Scene 5), but usually (as in Scene 12) it has to be discovered by the actors. It should be spoken accurately to keep the rhythm, not paraphrased. There is a single line to the left in the script where this is the case.

The play follows a general pattern in having scenes of dialogue in 'prose' interspersed with these scenes of more rhythmic 'surrealistic' dialogue which is designed to carry the story forward.

The original production was performed 'in promenade' with actors and audience sharing the same space (see diagram next page).

Chorus parts were played by members of the cast, and minor parts were doubled as below (the Headley Theatre Club cast in 2000):—

Matabel	Mel White
Jonas Kink, the Broomsquire	Tony Grant
Simon Verstage, landlord of The Ship Inn	David Irwin
Susanna Verstage, wife of Simon	Wendy Downs
Iver Verstage, their son	Peter Christopherson
Sarah Rocliffe, sister of Jonas	Pru Harrold
Giles Cheel, an elder broomsquire	Stan Sharp
Betsy Cheel, his wife	Linda Daruvala
Markham, a solicitor	Nick Webb
Barelegs, an attorney	Rod Sharp
Judge, at Kingston Crown Court	David Irwin
Defence Counsel	Linda Daruvala
Puttenham, Guardian of the Poor in Thursley	Stan Sharp
Doctor, staying at The Ship Inn	Linda Daruvala
Vicar of Thursley	Rod Sharp
The Sailor	Nick Webb
Casey, a murderer	Stan Sharp
Marshall, a murderer	Pru Harrold
Lonigon, a murderer	Linda Daruvala
Labourer 1	Rod Sharp
Labourer 2	Stan Sharp
Chorus	Linda Daruvala, David Irwin

Members of the audience were invited to play the roles of jurymen (selected during the interval), and given scripts to follow. It is up to Iver to ensure that they come to the right decision in Scene 22!

Cast members played live music at the wedding feast and at other points in the play where a passage of time is implied, and the play ended with a 'Grand Circle Dance' involving cast and audience.

The original set was designed to be portable on two trailers and able to be laid out within an hour at any location. Hessian was attached to wooden poles around the acting area to give a rustic effect and four 6-inch high triangular rostra were used at the corners to give raised acting areas. The actors entered the set by way of gaps in the hessian at the corners.

Thor's stone was made of chicken wire over a wooden frame and covered in painted hessian. The solid table was constructed to be strong enough for Jonas to stand on!

Looking towards Thor's Stone
as set up in Haslemere Museum, June 2013

Sketch for layout of the acting area.

*In the four corners we had 6" high triangular rostra,
given names as shown for actors' reference.*

*The acting area was surrounded by a hessian screen.
Audience sat inside around the edge, or shared the actors' furniture.
Cast entered through gaps at the corners of the screen.*

*The play starts and ends with Mrs V, Simon, Iver, Sarah & Jonas
standing in the corners and at the edge of the acting area to give a
stereo sound effect to the first and last few lines of the script.*

Pantomimes & Plays by John Owen Smith

Full length pantomimes (2 acts) with one interval:

- **Aladdin** The pantomime with the flying palace – 15 speaking parts + chorus

- **Ali Baba** Scheherazade introduces her very last Arabian Night's tale – 18 speaking parts + chorus

- **Cinderella** Baron Hardup's household as tradition tells it – with immortal lines – 14 speaking parts + chorus

- **Dick Whittington** and his cat – the tale as recorded by Fred Chaucer – 16 speaking parts + chorus

- **Humpty Dumpty** The Muffet Mob's on the loose – can old egghead save the day? – 16 speaking parts + 7 children speaking + chorus

- **Jack and the Beanstalk** Witch Whey's wicked wheeze won't work – will it? – 17 speaking parts + chorus

- **Nutcracker** The script Tchaikovsky might have set to music, if he'd known – 15 speaking parts + chorus

- **Puss in Boots** That talking cat gets everywhere – and gets his just desserts! – 15 speaking parts + chorus

- **Little Red Riding Hood** There could be a fete worse than death – ask the Wolf! – 16 speaking parts + chorus

- **Robin Hood** A cricket match in Sherwood Forest? There's Nun Better to play – 15 speaking parts + chorus

- **Sleeping Beauty** The show with an interval of a hundred years! – 11 speaking parts + chorus

- **Snow White and the 7 Dwarfs** The mirror's off the wall in more ways than one! – 18 speaking parts + chorus

Mini Pantomimes (in verse): **approx 15-20 mins run time**

- **Cinderelder** Prince Charming gets a bit fed up with Cinderella after 20 years! – 9 speaking parts

- **Bleeding Moody** Can you imagine the Sleeping Beauty as a teenager of today? – 6 speaking parts

Full length plays (2 acts) with one interval:

- **Flora's Heatherley** An historical play based on Flora Thompson's time in Grayshott 1898–1901 – 20 speaking parts

- **Flora's Peverel** An historical play based on Flora Thompson's time in Liphook 1916–1928 – 25 speaking parts

- **Riot!** – a dramatisation of the Selborne and Headley Workhouse Riots of 1830, plus historical notes – 30 speaking parts

- **MacHamlet** A Shakespearean comedy – 21 speaking parts

- **Bard Again!** MacHamlet takes to foreign parts – 21 speaking parts

- **MacHamlet Goes West!** and meets a Tempest – 23 speaking parts